I Have Nothing But Kids

How to Utilize Your Children's Ministry

A Children's Ministry Operational Manual

by

Elizabeth Paddy

How to Utilize Your Children's Ministry

Copyright © 2009
Elizabeth Paddy

All rights reserved. No part
of this book may be
reproduced
in any form, except for the
inclusion of brief quotations
in a review, without
permission in writing from
the author or publisher.

Library of Congress Card
Number:
ISBN: 978-0-578-06457-4

How to Utilize Your Children's Ministry

Additional copies can be obtained by contacting:

Elizabeth Paddy

PRINTED IN THE U.S.A.

How to Utilize Your Children's Ministry

TABLE OF CONTENTS

SECTION ONE

Pages

A Message from the Heart of Our Pastor
The Vision of Building Children's Ministry
Introduction to Children's Ministry
Children's Ministry Workers
Children's Ministry Structure

SECTION TWO

Pages

Family Day
Requirements of a Children's Ministry Worker
Children's Ministry Roles
Job Description of a Children's Pastor
Children's Ministry Teacher
Children's Ministry Supplies Coordinator
Resources
Praise and Worship Coordinator
Audio Ministry
Puppet / Drama Ministry Coordinator
The Victory Dollar Store Coordinator
Personal Ministry Workers
Costume Supervisors

SECTION THREE

Pages 29-40

How to Utilize Your Children's Ministry

New Worker's Information
Making Deposits into Future Generations
Teacher Development and Training Process
Why do We Minister to Children
Five Important Principles for Ministering to Children
Discipline in Children's Ministry
New Rules
Memory Verse Challenge
Children's Ministry Worker's Confession
Children Ministry Confession
Characteristics of Children
Creating Lesson that Impact Lives
How Learning Takes Place
Kidz for Jesus Ministries

TABLES OF CONTENTS (CONTINUED)

SECTION FOUR
                          Pages

Evangelism Ministry
Puppet Ministry
Choir Ministry

How to Utilize Your Children's Ministry

SECTION FIVE
Pages

Audio Ministry
Music Ministry
Prayer Ministry
Ushers Ministry

SECTION SIX
Pages

High Energy Level Games

About Elizabeth Paddy
Page

How to Utilize Your Children's Ministry

My desire is for this manual to bless you and hopefully save you a lot of time and research.

Section One

How to Utilize Your Children's Ministry

A MESSAGE FROM THE HEART OF OUR PASTOR

There are some things that are good and there are some things that are precious in the sight of God. Great faith, a meek and quiet attitude, and obedience are some of them.

One of the most overlooked, yet precious things to God are children. They may be little in stature, but big in mind and heart!! They are the leaders, preachers, and forecasters of the future and we must invest in training their spirit and mind. How soon we forget that we were "little people" too!

Jesus, in His busy schedule, took the time to lay His hands on children and bless them because He knew that they had to be guided and protected in the things of God.

Thank God that in this "selfish" and "me" age someone is taking the time to "bless" the children. This book will help you to be a better and more effective guide in leading children in the things of God.

In this book, my daughter, Elder Elizabeth Paddy will provide you with some tremendous insights that are easy to follow and use. It is a hands-on manual that will take your Children's project to another level. It has been proven and tested over time.

If we invest good things in the life of our Children, then we will reap a great harvest!

Dr. Bishop Jimmie A. Ellis III
Victory Christian Center

How to Utilize Your Children's Ministry

Dear Children's Ministry Workers,

This is our time to increase in Children's Ministry which has gone to a new level of excitement. **Kidz for Jesus** is a dream and vision manifested by God to give our children all the blessings God has for them. Our children can now run to impact this next generation of the unchurched, untaught and uncommitted.

Ministering to children is an assignment that Dr. Ellis does not take lightly. Because of Bishop Ellis' never-ending faithfulness and overwhelming generosity, the children encounter an exciting and positive learning experience when they attend Sunday and Mid-Week Church in Motion Bible Study.

I know that it is time to prepare the next generation in the things of God and give them a solid foundation in the Word of God. Children need to know that God gave us a book filled with wisdom to help them understand life today. His message provides truths they won't find anywhere else.

This manual will assist in communicating the vision, policies and procedures of

How to Utilize Your Children's Ministry

Children's Ministry, as well as give your workers the assistance they need to be effective. I believe that God has equipped us with the necessary gifts, talents, and skills that will cause us to build and further the work of this ministry and the vision of pastors nationwide.

Children's Ministry workers give 100% of their time in making sure that when a child leaves the Sunday school classroom, they've had an experience that will encourage their family and friends to want a relationship with Jesus. Children's Ministry workers know that whatever they make happen for others God will make happen for them.

Together, we can do as the Bible instructs us in **Proverbs 22:6. "Train up a child in the way he should go and when he is old, he will not depart from it."** Your commitment as a Godly example and instructor to the children, will equip them with the necessary tools to take their rightful place in the Body of Christ today and in days to come.

In His Service,

Elder Elizabeth Paddy

Introduction

It is clearly stated in the Bible… **"Where there is no vision, the people will perish."** The Bible also admonishes us to **"…write the vision down and make it plain upon tablets so that he that readeth it may run with it…"**

The Children's Ministry is designed to meet the needs of children ages 6-11. Workers are trained to minister the Word of God at the level of understanding for the appropriate age. It is the primary goals of Children's Ministry to teach and instill in the children the Seven Biblical Principles of Abundant Living and Christian values. The principles are Salvation, Authority of the Believer, Prayer, The Holy Spirit, Healing Faith and Prosperity. In Children's Ministry there are two different services designed for teaching and impacting this generation: Sunday Service and Church in Motion Bible Study. Children's Ministry has established monthly goals for each child that will give them a strong spiritual foundation for daily life. Our goals are for each child to be proficient in the following areas:

- Scriptural references for Salvation, Baptism with the Holy Spirit, and Water baptism
- Locate and say Books of the Bible with boldness
- Recite the Beatitudes and Ten Commandments
- Memorize and recite memory verses and Mid-week scriptures
- Know scripture references for salvation, healing, prayer, prosperity and faith
- Know scriptural references for leading another person to salvation

The Children's Ministry was established to fulfill the mandate God has given you to build people of purpose, power and praise. It is our responsibility to create an environment for our children to hear God's voice. We want our children to know God's purpose for their lives and to be free to worship and praise Him in spirit and in truth. Our children are a priority to us. As children workers, our responsibility is to teach the Godly principles that will give our children the Biblical foundation and knowledge of who God is. We must teach our children the things of God and train them to share Jesus with others, wherever they are.

INTRODUCTION to CHILDREN'S MINISTRY

There are several different areas of participation for everyone in Children's Ministry. There is a place especially for **You!** We are a team of Teachers, Administrative Assistant, Musicians, A Teacher Development Team, Awesome the Clown, Resource Managers, Audio and Video persons, Props Team, Data Entry Team, Curriculum Writers, Drama Team, Storytellers, Costumed Characters, Puppet handlers, Artist, Event Planners and Designers fulfilling a mandate from God, for this ministry to build children of **PURPOSE, POWER AND PRAISE.**

We are committed to give you sufficient training to master all of the areas above. However, we do request that each team member complete every aspect of training and be proficient in all areas of Children's Ministry, just in case you are ever called upon to fill in for someone. We believe that each of us have individual gifts and talents that will enhance Children's Ministry. It is important that you know ***Children's Ministry is a vital part of your Ministry.***

How to Utilize Your Children's Ministry

CHILDREN'S MINISTRY STRUCTURE

Children's Ministry worship services are designed to teach children age 6 through 11 how to understand the Bible and worship God at their level. The Children's Ministry worship services parallels the adult worship services in the following elements:

- Praise and Worship at all levels
- Puppet and Drama Skits
- Storytelling
- Games with memory verse
- Chat Time (where children have an opportunity to discuss)
- Salvation
- Communion
- School concerns
- Learn to pry for themselves and others
- Children's Confession
- Teacher's Confession
- Financial Faith Confession
- Names of God Confession
- Recognition of First-Time Visitors
- Prayer Request
- Ministry of the Word

- Offerings
- Altar Call
- Object Lessons
- Games and Loads of Fun

Church in Motion

Church in Motion (CIM) Bible study services incorporates a variety of activities to enhance the Biblical foundation we wish to establish in our children's lives. Other activities are implemented during Church in Motion services such as:

- Story night
- Arts and Crafts
- Movie night
- Activity night
- Game night

Children also learn assigned scriptures each week with lots of other fun activities. You will not be bored. Each week children receive a Victory Dollar for learning the Mid-Week scripture and Ram Ticket for bring a friend to CIM.

1st WEEK OF EVERY MONTH – ARTS AND CRAFTS NIGHT

The Banquet Hall in Children's Ministry becomes little workshops. Children of all ages participate making crafts that are applicable to the lesson. The crafts are age appropriate and the teachers work along with the students to complete the crafts.

2nd WEEK OF EVERY MONTH – STORY NIGHT

A costumed instructor will tell a fictional story, or read a Bible story from a storybook that relates to the central Truth of Sunday's lesson. Involving the children in the story is also a mechanism to reinforce the lesson. If given the opportunity to do the lesson, the children will retain more of the information being taught.

3rd WEEK OF EVERY MONTH – MOVIE NIGHT

In this age of video technology, we have developed additional ways of reinforcing the lesson through video. On Movie Night, viewing secular and Christian videos are used to reinforce the lesson. The children view a video that is somewhat based upon the theme of the lesson and the instructor ties the video and the lesson together.

4th WEEK OF EVERY MONTH - GAME NIGHT

During Game night, the children play a variety of fun games such as: The Donut Game, The Word if Right, Run for Jesus, Bible Bingo, and The Balloon Stomp, etc. Games are also effective in defining and practicing character virtue.

CIM Live is an exciting time of fellowship with Children's Ministry.

How to Utilize Your Children's Ministry

Section Two

FAMILY DAY

Pastor Jim has designated Family Day to be on the 5th Sunday of the month. On Family Day, there is no Children's Ministry for ages 3-11. The children perform during worship service. Parents are encouraged to spend this Sunday in worship as a family. This allows our children several different opportunities: (1) the children become accustomed to being in adult worship services; (2) the children are able to see their parents worshipping God; and (3) the children become acquainted with our Pastor and visionary, Dr. Jimmie A. Ellis III.

SPECIAL SERVICES / SEMINARS

The Bishop will host a conference, seminar or some other form of Special Services. Children's Ministry is normally provided for special services. When we have special services, we allow workers to sign up by making a commitment to serve in these services. Those workers will receive a CD of the seminar or conference.

THE VICTORY DOLLAR STORE

The Victory Dollar Store is designed to reward the children for their faithfulness. During CIM/Midweek service, boys and girls have the opportunity to receive Victory dollars for saying assigned scripture and bringing their Bibles. The children can receive up to twenty Victory Dollars for being friends to service. This allows our children to learn about discipleship for the Kingdom of God.

MEMORY VERSE CHALLENGE

We want our children in Children's Ministry to work very hard to memorize memory verses each month and we want to reward them. The reward will also encourage other children to memorize the verses. The memory verses are important because it helps children know what the Word of God says and then they are able to apply it in their lives. We want to be consistent in the way we reward the children for memorizing the memory verses. Children will say their memory verses to monitor wearing Memory Verse Badges for Victory Dollars. The following has been implemented to carry out this exciting time of learning God's Word.

How to Utilize Your Children's Ministry

Victory Dollars should be distributed as follows:

If a child knows 2 complete memory verses, 4 Victory Dollars are rewarded.

If a child knows 1 memory verse, 2 Victory Dollars are rewarded.

Children can receive 5 Victory Dollars for being a friend and 20 Victory Dollars for bringing 5 friends.

1. No memory verse sheets are to be handed out on the Sunday of Memory Verse Challenge. The child must be able to recite the scripture from memory.
2. In order to receive a Victory Dollar for reciting a scripture, the child must know the verse and the scripture reference. You may give the child the first word of the scripture to get them on track, but no other coaching should be given. Once a child begins to say a verse, it must be completed.
3. Monitors should wear the Memory Verse badges so that the children can easily identify them.

REQUIREMENTS OF A CHILDREN'S MINISTRY WORKER

- Faithfulness and punctuality is a requirement for Children's Ministry workers. All workers are to arrive 30 minutes before their scheduled services.

How to Utilize Your Children's Ministry

- We would like for workers to commit to a Sunday, and a mid-week service.
- Attend church services when not volunteering in Children's Ministry.
- For special services we need Children's Ministry workers to volunteer to work in Children's Ministry.
- Criminal background and child abuse clearance.
- Provide a working phone number and email address or the Children's Ministry Directory.
- Be committed to creating an authentic church experience that exceeds all expectations for Children's Ministry.

RESIGNATIONS

If you decide you are unable to continue your duties as a Children's Ministry worker, or reasons of your choice, we ask that you submit a 30-day resignation notice to the Children's Ministry Coordinator.

RESPONSIBILITIES OF CHILDREN'S MINISTRY WORKERS

Having the Love of God and wanting to empower the children of this generation with a spiritual foundation, is one of the many reasons why volunteers become involved in Children's Ministry. Our primary objective is to make every child feel welcome and important, knowing that God perfects those things which concerns them. The goal in Children's Ministry is for children to walk out and say "Wow"! the Bible is such a smart book. We must teach simple. If kids don't understand verbiage used, the lesson is lost with no hope for application.

Our purpose in Children's Ministry is to help build children of Purpose by introducing salvation to every child. Salvation is the tool needed to be saved. Power is the next step of empowerment. The children are given the opportunity to receive the Baptism with the Holy Spirit, with the evidence of speaking in their prayer language. Praise sets the tone for the children to be ministered to.

Punctuality, dedication and faithfulness are requirements or all Children's Ministry workers.

As a worker, you are an example to the children. Being involved in the Children's Ministry service allows the children to see you worship God and take part in action songs.

Be mindful that the assigned workers are there to help control discipline and order.

We ask all workers to pray for the service the children and those people who are in charge of ministering to the children. Being sensitive to the leading and prompting of the Spirit can make a big difference in the accomplishments of the service.

Be mindful that God is not a God of disorder. Everything that we do is done decently and in order.

CHILDREN'S MINISTRY ROLES

There are various positions in Children's Ministry.

JOB DESCRIPTION OF A CHILDREN'S PASTOR

Ephesians 4:11-12 And He gave some, apostles; and some, prophets; and some, evangelists; and some, pastors and teachers; or the perfecting of the saints, for the work of the ministry, for edifying of the body of Christ.

The role of a children's pastor can be divided into four areas. The first role or purpose is to pastor the children of the local church.

In ministering to children and teachers, I've heard people ask, "Why do we need a children's pastor? We have teachers ministering to our children." In **Ephesians 4**, it states that one of the purposes of the five-fold ministry is to edify the body of Christ. Children are a part of the body of Christ and need to be ministered to also.

Notice in verse 11, Jesus not only gave teachers, but he also gave pastors to the body of Christ. In W.E. Vine's Expository Dictionary of New Testament Words, defines the word, pastor, as "a shepherd, one who tends, herds or flocks, (not one who merely feeds them)."

A pastor's ministry is more than just teaching or feeding. It involves training and nurturing the sheep, from baby lambs, until they become strong Christians. A pastor gives people an opportunity to do what they've learned rather than just teaching them.

The children of the local church need to be pastored, not just taught! The pastor of the church cannot effectively minister to adults and children. The pastor cannot get up on Sunday morning and preach to the adults for 15 minutes and then say, "Wait a minute, folks" and then run to Children's Church and preach to the children for 15 minutes. You, as a children's pastor are an extension of our pastor's ministry within the local church.

Jesus is the Chief Shepherd, and the pastor is an under-shepherd, under Jesus. Jesus is not here in person therefore; He gave the pastor as a gift to the local church to pastor the sheep. The pastor is an extension of Jesus' ministry because Jesus cannot personally pastor every sheep. The pastor needs to be in constant communication with the Chief Shepherd (Jesus) to find out what direction the church is supposed to be going.

The children's pastor is an under-shepherd under the pastor, because the pastor cannot effectively reach all age groups. The pastor is the head of the church and the children's pastor is an extension of the pastor's ministry. Therefore, the children's pastor needs to be in constant communication with the pastor, to find out what direction the church is going.

As a children's pastor, you will need to be with the children on a regular basis. Part of your job is to set an example in front of the children of a Godly lifestyle. Peter exhorts the elders in 1Peter 5:2-3 Feed the flock of God which is among you taking the oversight thereof, "not by constraint, bgut willing; not for filthy lucre, but of a ready mind; Neither as being lords over God's heritage, but being examples to the flock.

The word "example" in Webster's Dictionary means a person or thing worthy of imitation. Children learn by imitation. That's the way God created them. You can't tell children, "Do as I do." They need to have a lifestyle set in front of them of someone who is worthy of imitation. The children's pastor has to be living an upright life and he/she has to be with the children on a regular basis.

In pasturing children, you will have to feed them the Word of God on a level that their minds can understand. You can't just get up and preach from the Bible to kids like you would to adults. Their spirits will pick things up, but their mind will not understand. Jesus said, **"When anyone heareth the word of the kingdom, and UNERSTANETH IT NOT, then cometh the wicked one, and SNATCHETH AWAY that which was SOWN IN HIS HEART." (Matthew 13:19)**

When preaching to children, you need to use puppets, visual aids, acting skits or anything that will make the Bible real to children. Kids don't need to be taught to believe God for the house payment, buy you can teach them how to believe God for a bicycle.

As a children's pastor, you will also have to train children to do things that they've learned in Children's Church. **"Go then and make disciples of all nations, baptizing them in the name of the Father, and the Son, and the Holy Spirit." (Matthew 28:19 Amplified).**

The heart of a pastor is discipleship, just like the heart of an evangelist is soul winning. We need the evangelist to win the lost and we need the pastor to disciple the lambs from spiritual babes to mature Christians.

Jesus taught the multitudes, but He pastured the twelve disciples. Jesus spent special time with the disciples and when they were mature, He sent them forth and said, **"Heal the sick, cleanse the lepers, raise the dead, cast out devils, freely ye have received, freely give." (Matthew 8:10)**

As children's pastors, a big part of our job is to train children to do what we have taught them.

Several years ago, I was complaining to the Lord, because I didn't have enough faithful workers to do a quality puppet skit. The Lord spoke to my heart saying, "Train the children." I obeyed the Lord and I discovered that children are the greatest untapped ministry resources in our churches today.

Presently, we have five organized ministries in our Children's Church to train tomorrow's leaders today!

PUPPET MINISTRY

Children involved on the puppet team are responsible for puppet skits during all of our Children's Church services.

MUSIC MINISTRY

These children are trained to lead the Sunday morning worship service in Children's Church. Sometimes getting kids to sing and worship God is like pulling teeth; but when they see their peers excited about worshipping God, they get excited.

PRAYER MINISTRY

The prayer ministry meets every Sunday morning to pray for Children's Church services. We are training these children to be might warriors.

USHER MINISTRY

We are training the Children's Church ushers to serve God in the ministry of helps. They take up the offering and are responsible for the appearance of the Children's Church.

AUDIO VISUAL

These children run all of the sound and video equipment during our Children's Church services. They are responsible for taking proper care of all microphones and any other equipment that is used.

Over 50% of the ministry in Children's Church is conducted by children. Praise the Lord!

Start asking the Lord what you can do to disciple the children in your children's ministry. Don't think that you have to start all of these ministries at one time. Pick one ministry and start with that one. Pray and believe God to send you the people to help you fulfill your ministry to the children.

Not only do you have to meet the spiritual needs of the children; but as a children's pastor, it is part of your responsibility to see their social and practical needs are met. Some churches have the attitude that all they are supposed to do is to teach the Word; but children (especially teenagers) are naturally social. They have social and practical needs as well as spiritual needs. If their social needs are not met by the church, they will look to the world to meet those needs.

About once a month, try to have an activity for the children. There is a lot you can do with them. For example: roller skating, hayrides, camp outs, swimming, zoo trips, etc. Some people will say that it's not important to do these activities; but it is important.

The second role or purpose of a children's pastor is to recruit and train children's ministry workers. One of the biggest questions in churches today is how do we get enough workers in our children's ministry?"

RECRUITING WORKERS FOR THE CHILDREN'S MINISTRY

Step 1: Set an Example of Quality in the Children's Ministry. The church will judge the children's ministry by how the pastor represents it. The children's pastor needs to set a quality example in every area including: dress, appearance, conversation, life style and ministry.

Romans 11:13 reads: **For I speak to you Gentiles, in as much as I am the apostle of the Gentiles, I magnify my office."** Paul said that he magnified his office. He didn't magnify himself but he did magnify the office that God called him to. As a children's pastor you need to magnify your office. As you do, it will cause other people to be desirous of it. Never get up in front of the church and beg for workers.

Some people, in an effort to get new workers, will say things like, "We need help. It's hard work over there working with those kids. You just don't know what it's like. Please, if just a few of you could help it would really mean a lot." If that is how you present the children's ministry, everyone will say, "I don't want to go over there."

Whenever you present the children's ministry to your church you need to magnify your office. Share with the people testimonies about how God has ministered to the children. Think of what you are doing as something important. You are there to meet the needs of those kids. If you don't think it is important, then no one else will.

1Chronicles 11:10-24 talks about David's men lifted up his spear against three hundred and he slew them. David's might men were capable of destroying a whole army, yet Saul didn't have any men like this. How did David get men like these? He drew them. David was just like them himself. David was a quality person, and he drew "quality people" to himself. As you determine to set a quality example, you will draw quality people to you, to get the job done.

Step 2: Look for People who are Faith and Have Good Attitudes. Don't just look for the people who are talented or may have ability. A right attitude is the most important attribute when looking for workers.

A good leader is someone who can develop the ability in others when there is nothing to be seen on the surface. Start with people who don't have any talent but who are faithful. Train and develop their talent. Draw it out of them. People themselves feel as if you owe them something if they help you. People themselves feel as if you owe them something if they help you. People you've trained and developed will always be faithful to your ministry. You may ask, "How do I develop ability in others?"

Step 3: Learn how to Lead People. The first thing you need to do with your workers is to let them know what you expect out of them. Set a standard of excellence; but don't expect excellence from them at the beginning. When people first start working in the children's ministry, don't use harsh correcting words. Use encouraging words.

A shepherd doesn't drive a flock, he leads it. If your workers hear nothing but correction without encouraging words, they will think they aren't doing anything right. They won't follow you very long.

A good leader can always put himself in the shoes of the people underneath him. When a leader makes a decision, he can think, "How will this affect the people working with me?" Some "leaders" just say, "I'm the boss and this is the way it's going to be." A true leader believes in the people working with him and he always has their interest at heart. Be encouraging to your people. Always build them up. People do better when they feel good about themselves. Remember to set an example of quality. Look for people who are faithful; rather than having great ability. Learn to lead people.

<u>REACH THE PARENTS OF THE CHILDREN</u>

You might teach the kids one or two days every week; but their parents are teaching them seven days a week. If the parents don't see the vision for what you are doing then a lot of what you do becomes a waste.

Step 1: Establish communication between the children's ministry and the parents. Inform the parents what you are teaching their children so they can reinforce the same message at home.

Deuteronomy 6:6-7 states: Memorize his laws and tell them to your children over and over again. Talk about them all the time, whether you are at home or walking along the road or going to bed at night or getting up in the morning. (CEV) Children learn from repetition. They don't get the message, just because we preach it one time in Children's Church. The principles that will really stick with your children are the ones that are reinforced at home.

According to **Deuteronomy 6,** the main responsibility of raising children rests upon the parents. The Word of God also instructs the church to preach the gospel to every creature. I believe when the church and the home are working together we have a powerful team that will train up our children to be strong men and women of God.

Step 2: Preach the Word to their children. If you are ministering the Word to their children then it will come out at home. Don't just entertain the kids; minister to them. Your job is not to keep the kids going until your pastor is finished. Your job is to minister to those kids.

Step 3: Show honor and respect toward the parents. When the parents come to the door to drop off or pick up their kids, smile and treat them with kindness. Even if the parents are rude to you, remember to show love. When you show honor to them, they will show honor back to you.

Step 4: Magnify your office. Paul said in **Romans 11:13** that he magnified his office. It's wrong to magnify yourself but God want you to magnify the office He has called you to. You might ask, "How do I magnify my office?" Dress sharp! Don't preach in blue jeans and tennis shoes. You should not dress any differently ministering to children than you would if you were ministering to adults. Make sure your room looks neat and organized. If something is important to you than other people will think it's important also.

Remember to establish communication with the parents. Occasionally do a program in front of the church. Preach the Word to your Children's church. Show honor to the parents and magnify your office. As you do these steps, you will reach the parents and the children will benefit greatly.

ESTABLISH AN EFFECTIVE RELATIONSHIP WITH YOUR PASTOR

It is of vital importance that the pastor of the church has a vision for children's ministry. The children's ministry in your church will not grow beyond your pastor's vision for it because God will not override the authority He has placed there.

Step 1: Show honor to him/her and submit yourself to his ministry. The pastor is the head of the local church ad anything with more than one head is a freak.

Step 2: Have a positive attitude. Don't always come to your pastor with problems. If you come to him with problems, that is what he will think about whenever he see you. When problems arise, deal with them yourself. Come to him with good reports. Make sure you have more good reports to share with your pastor than negative things.

Remember, submit yourself to your pastor's ministry and show honor to him. Bear fruit in areas that are important to him. Deal with things in the spiritual realm and always maintain a positive attitude. As you do these steps the children's ministry in your church will prosper.

NEW WORKERS INFORMATION

Now that you have decided to build your own Children's Ministry, you will need a dedicated team of workers that God will use to impact the lives of the children. It will benefit the Children's Ministry if you organize monthly workshops, hire new workers to receive teacher development training sessions. These sessions will deal with every area of Children's Ministry because new workers should receive hands-on activities for ministering to the children along with a Teacher's Manual that explains how Children's Ministry operates.

New workers should be assigned to a team leader to complete observations of classes in the Children's Ministry. They should be given the opportunity to observe lessons being taught along with object lessons, memory verses, and lots of fun activities within the classroom. They should also be given an opportunity to observe the administrative assistant and supplies coordinators as these are vital roles in the Children's Ministry.

Key Roles and Responsibilities of Workers

Children's Ministry Teacher

The Children's Ministry teacher is responsible for the overall class an orderly presentation of all lessons. The teacher is knowledgeable and prepared to teach the lesson. The teacher is fervent in prayer for the needs of the children and the Children's Ministry. The tea here communicates on a regular basis with the Children's Ministry team leader. The teacher:

- Attends workshops;
- Attends Intercessory prayer;
- Reports any incident that may occur in the classroom

- Keeps the children excited during and after his/her lessons; and
- Responsible for encouraging the students to study God's Word.

Children's Ministry Team Leader

The Children's Ministry Team Leader is responsible for the weekly functions of a designated service. The Team Leader assists the Coordinator by observing and accessing the teachers in the classroom, training new teachers, scheduling team members for general assembly and following guidelines under authority.

- Is the primary contact person in case of emergencies or incidents;
- Is responsible for handling any discipline challenges that occur;
- Is responsible for making sure Children's Ministry workers function with no discord;
- Is responsible for communicating with the administrative assistant and coordinators; and
- Is responsible for attending all workshops and Team Leader meetings

Children's Ministry Coordinator

The Children's Ministry coordinator is responsible for the implementation of the Ministry's vision. The coordinator oversees the administrative duties. The coordinator develops a unified team of administrative assistants and teaching support. The coordinator is ultimately responsible for developing and training all Children's Ministry workers. Other areas of responsibility for the coordinator include special events and any activities that may be assigned to Children's Ministry as it relates to the vision of the Church. The coordinator should perform duties such as:

- Maintaining a database of all children;
- Creating and maintaining the events calendar;
- Submitting a monthly report of attendance, water baptism and enrollment; and
- Following up with parents regarding their child's behavior.

Children's Ministry Administrative Assistant

How to Utilize Your Children's Ministry

The Children's Ministry administrative assistant is responsible for handling the administrative duties for Sunday and Church in Motion services. The administrative assistant is a vital part of the overall operation. He/she must be familiar with every aspect of Children's Ministry. He/she works closely with the Coordinator and communicates on a weekly basis. The administrative assistant should perform duties such as:

- Assisting with signing children in and out of service;
- Making sure all parents of children with special needs complete and receive the necessary information; and
- Responsible for working with the teens during services.

Children's Ministry Supplies Coordinator

The Children's Ministry Supplies Coordinator's primary function is to maintain supplies and/or matter is needed in Children's Ministry. The Supplies Coordinator must have all items available for teachers before each service. The Supplies Coordinator will submit an inventory supply list to the Children's

Ministry Coordinator each month. Other duties may include:

- Setting up each classroom with items the teacher requests;
- Requesting and maintaining an inventory list for supplies needed in the Children's Ministry;
- Keeping inventory of the snacks that are provided for each service in the supply room;
- Assisting teachers with restroom breaks; and
- Making sure the offering for Sunday service is picked up by assigned treasurer.

Praise and Worship Coordinator

The Praise and Worship Coordinator is responsible for selecting praise and worship songs. The Praise and Worship Coordinator also assigns and auditions praise-team singers for each service. He/she gathers the worship motivators for the children (shakers, tambourines, sticks, pom-poms, etc.)

Audio Personnel

The Audio Personnel are responsible for the operation and maintenance of the sound system and other media equipment. Audio personnel are responsible for the set-up and disassembling of all audio equipment including microphones, tape players, etc.

Section Three

MAKING DEPOSITS INTO FUTURE GENERATIONS

The world of Children's Ministry is exciting and I am honored that you have chosen to allow God to stretch you in this area of ministry. You have made a quality decision in making deposits into the lives of children. It's very rewarding to bring children to the saving knowledge of Christ and contribute to their spiritual growth on a consistent basis.

Here are a few benefits of being part of a Children's Ministry:

- The **benefit of belonging** to a local church where your basic spiritual needs can be met.
- The **benefit of developing** through teaching the Word of God to children and watching them grow and understand their spiritual responsibilities.

How to Utilize Your Children's Ministry

- The **benefit of sharing** this experience with other teachers, parents and students.
- The **benefit of knowing** the peace that comes when you are an active part in helping build the Kingdom of God.

<u>TEACHER DEVELOPMENT and TRAINING PROCESS</u>

The purpose of the teacher development and training is to develop and enhance the teaching skills of the Children's Ministry team. This training is ongoing and should effectively influence creative ways for teaching the Word of God. The measurable objective is to see the training process increase the number of involved Children's Ministry workers and to see the victories and successes in the lives of the children as result of the teaching received from trained workers.

Once a worker receives approval for Children's Ministry, the worker will go through a three-month training stream, which will include attending sessions based on the various topics listed below. I suggest that all topics listed below be completed through observation and attendance to workshops in order for the new worker to begin teaching in the Children's Ministry.

Teacher Development Topics:

- **Introduction to Children's Ministry**
  This session welcomes the new worker and details why it is important to minister to children. Workers are given forms to fill out and will receive a call to schedule their training.

- **Children's Ministry Services and Administration**
  The new worker should attend a Children's Ministry service where he/she will be actively involved in the Praise and Worship service for the children. The new worker is expected to observe all aspects of the service, i.e., Welcome, Offering, Object Lesson and Prayer. The new worker is accompanied by a team leader and given a tour of the Children's Ministry. The new worker is given the opportunity to see the administration of the Children's

How to Utilize Your Children's Ministry

Ministry and the value it has in the lives of children.

- **Planning and Organizing**
  Your lesson must be well planned to meet the needs of the children. This topic teaches the workers to utilize time management in order to prepare a lesson.

- **Discipline in the Classroom**
  This session teaches the workers how to establish the expectations in the classroom in order to maintain discipline. Children will be removed from the classroom by a Team Leader if misbehavior continues.

- **Object Lessons**
  An object lesson is any tangible object(s) that can be used to creatively and effectively present and reinforce your lesson or memory verse.

- **Creative ways of Teaching**
  To be creative in teaching, you must know the material that you are teaching. Have fun activities that will involve the entire class. Keep

the lesson exciting. Remember, your enthusiasm while presenting the lesson will be contagious. Therefore, allow time for your students to share their thoughts with the class. This will help you to evaluate and/or improve your techniques.

- **Making the Appeals**
  When you give an invitation for children to be saved or to receive the Baptism with the Holy Spirit or to be water baptized, you must remember to be very clear. Information must be given step-by-step and on the level of the child's understanding. We must teach children that they are saved, according to the scripture in **Romans 10:9.**

- **Drama, Role Play, Arts and Crafts, Storytelling, Puppet Activities**
  Activities provide opportunities for children to gain understanding of scripture as well as application of Biblical concepts. Activities also allow children to get hands-on experience in making crafts about the Word of God. Telling a story about will help to illustrate your

theme, many like windows allow you to look inside a house. Role-play and Puppet skits make drama an exciting kind of Bible learning activity.

- **Fun and Game Activities**
  Playing games will allow the children to review the information that they have learned. Games offer help to accomplish this task and are used to encourage memorization of lessons and Bible verses.

EXPECTATIONS

Behavior is essential for learning in any environment. As workers, we have to maintain the discipline within the classroom without getting the focus off the Word of God. This includes knowing when to remove a child and when not to. Please refer to the section on Effective Discipline. Please remember the following expectations of all children in Children's Ministry: Never read or have children recite 4 or more rules.

How to Utilize Your Children's Ministry

The Key is for children to obey all the following rules!

1. To HAVE FUN!
2. I will raise my hand and be recognized by the teacher before speaking.
3. I will go to the restroom before service.
4. I will keep my hands, feet and other objects to myself.
5. I will be very quiet when the teacher is ministering salvation and the baptism with the Holy Spirit.
6. I will remain in my seat unless the teacher instructs me otherwise.
7. I will speak language that is acceptable to God.
8. I will refer to people by their name only.
9. I will respect my teacher.
10. Remember Rule No. 1, HAVE FUN!

In addition to the classroom expectations, Team Leaders and Administrative Assistants are available to assist the teachers. The following expectations should apply at all times.

How to Utilize Your Children's Ministry

1. No running in the building at any time.
2. No fighting or rough play.
3. Remind the children to go to the restroom and get a drink of water before class begins. NO ONE should be allowed to leave the classroom once class begins (unless it is a case of an emergency or a medical problem). If a child asks to go to the restroom, tell they will have to wait a few minutes. If they return to ask again, they are probably serious. Never allow children of any age to go to the restroom or get a drink of water alone.
4. Boys are not to wear hats in the classroom at any time.
5. Do not allow the children to chew gum in the classroom.
6. Encourage all children to stand during the worship service.
7. Keep your eyes and ears open at all times for potential problems (kicking, hitting, talking and playing with toys).

There are four (4) important rules you can have children recite:

1. Obey all Rules
2. Do not try to speak without a Microphone.
3. Do not get out of your seat without Permission.
4. You must have a Name Tag.

MEMORY VERSE CHALLENGE

On the 4th Sunday of each month, Children's Ministry will have Memory Verse Challenge. The purpose of this is to encourage the children to learn the Word of God. Workers will be assigned to wear badges that read, "I Can Listen to Your Memory Verse." These people will listen to the children recite their assigned memory verse from the Children's Ministry Policy on Memory Verse Challenge.

CREATING LESSONS THAT IMPACT LIVES

How to Utilize Your Children's Ministry

In this training session, you will learn to unlock the creativity on the inside of you. You will discover how children learn and how to create lessons that children will not forget.

The creative process is taking things that you already know and making them into something new and fresh.

As teachers in the Body of Christ, we have an extremely important role. We must represent God in the earth, walking upright before children, being a Godly example, setting the standard of excellence and live in obedience of God's Word. Because you have chosen to serve in one of the most rewarding Ministry Helps groups, you are an intricate part in building children of PURPOSE, POWER, and PRAISE! Determine that you will do your very best to teach children the ways of God and His purpose for their lives.

You must take the time to prepare and study your lesson. God can do more to inspire your creativity when you have absorbed the information prior to attempting to teach it.

The information that follows should give a good foundation for unleashing your own creativity and creating lessons that will influence the lives of children.

God was a creative teacher and He can inspire your creativity. It is important that you know how children retain information received.

How Learning Takes Place

Children will remember:
- 10% of what they HEAR
- 15% of what they SEE
- 20% of what they HEAR and SEE
- 40% of what they DISCUSS
- 80% of what they DO
- 90% of what they TEACH OTHERS

It is a mistake to think that just because you have taught the central theme of a lesson once the children will become bored because they have heard it before. We are designed to learn through repetition.

GENERAL GUIDELINES

1. Come to the service prayed up. The leading of the Lord is just as important in

How to Utilize Your Children's Ministry

ministering to children as it is in ministering to adults. The Holy Spirit will minister to children and you need to be prepared by being prayed up and full of the Word.

2. Report to the children's pastor for instructions.

3. Make sure you have an adequate supply of tracts (salvation and baptism in the Holy Spirit) available for the service.

4. Allow yourself enough time to set up any props needed.

5. Wear name tags at all times during services that you are on duty.

6. Report to Children's Church no later than 30 minutes prior to the start of the service.

7. Dress code: Look Sharp! We are representing the Lord Jesus Christ to the children.

How to Utilize Your Children's Ministry

Men: Suit coat or a dress shirt, slacks and a tie.
Ladies: Dress, skirt and blouse.

8. Personal Hygiene:
   Clean breath – use breath mints, please.
   Clean-shaven or neatly trimmed beards or mustaches.
   Hair neatly groomed.

9. Greet the children and let them know we love them. Be watchful for first time visitors.

10. After greeting children, seat them as they come in. Always fill the front rows first. Use discretion when seating children. *Example: Seating a large group of boys together could cause problems later during the service.*

11. No children are allowed in ministry area (front of the room) or behind the puppet stage unless specifically

requested by the teacher in charge.

12. You will be given an area to monitor. Always keeps one eye on the children and one eye on the teacher. The teacher sometimes point to a problem that you will have to deal with.

13. Problems with the children will be handled in the following manner:

- Speak to them to turn around, be quiet, etc.
- If you need to speak to them again, move them to a different seat.
- If they continue to be a problem, give them a warning.
- After receiving a warning, if they continue to be a problem, move them next to a staff member

- If the same child continues to be a problem on a regular basis, report him/her.

14. Do not carry on a friendly conversation with any of the children during the service. If you speak to one of them, it will be to correct or instruct them. The time to be friendly with them is before or after the service.

15. Gum chewing is not allowed in Children's Church.

16. Do not allow children to bring toys into Children's Church. If you see a child with a toy or any other object other than a Bible or purse, hold it for him or her until after Children's Church is over.

KIDZ for JESUS SERVICE

1. ***Spiritual Aerobics*** – the Children's Team Leaders will

lead the children through a series of exercises. The purpose of this is to warm the children up for praise and worship. It gets them moving.

2. ***Worship*** – the worship leader will teach the children how to offer praise and worship to the Lord ad why this done. Worship is the believer's number one priority, children included.

3. ***Teach the Word*** – everything said and done in Children's Church should be centered around the goal of putting the Word into the children on their level.

4. ***Maintain order and control at all times*** – God is not the author of confusion. The assistant teachers and helpers are responsible for taking care of disturbances and maintaining control of the children during the service. This will allow the teacher to

do a more effective job of ministering the Word.

If a child has a need, he/she will raise their hand. Their questions are to be answered by the assistant teachers and helpers; not the Pastor. Maintaining control is especially important during altar all where any unnecessary disturbance may keep a child from receiving Jesus or getting any of their needs met.

AFTER SERVICE

1. Pick up trash and straighten the chairs.
2. Place lost articles in the proper place.
3. Make sure the room is tidy in the event it is scheduled to be used.

COUNSELING GUIDELINES

I. SALVATION

How to Utilize Your Children's Ministry

- Present your invitation to Salvation.
- Have everyone bow their heads ad close their eyes.
- Ask how many boys and girls have Jesus in their hearts. Ask the children to raise their hand.
- Ask how many children don't have Jesus in their hearts and they want Him. Ask the children to raise their hand.
- Have those who raised their hand to stand up by their chair.
- Have them come to the front.
- Build up the children who come forward by letting them know that this is the most important decision they have made.
- Take the children to another room to be counseled.
- When the children are gathered in your counseling room, take control. Do not let them become unruly. Build them up.
- Explain to the children that you will ask everyone a question. "Why did you come back here?" You are trying to locate if they know what they are doing. "Have

you ever asked Jesus into your heart or are you born again?"

- If a child says they have been born again, we do not pray the Prayer of Salvation with them again. We explain that once Jesus has come into our heart, He will never leave us. If we disobey, we ask for forgiveness (sometimes children are convicted by disobedience they have done). They need to know they just have to ask for forgiveness. We then pray with them thanking the Father for them, etc.
- During the screening process, separate the children. Separate those who you'll pray the Prayer of Salvation with. The others put in another area of the room. When the screening is complete, release those who you will not pray with back into the service.

Guidelines for the Prayer of Salvation are found in **Romans 10:9-10**.

- Confess with your mouth Jesus Christ is Lord.
- Believe in your heart that God raised Jesus from the dead.

How to Utilize Your Children's Ministry

- Believe by faith that you are saved.

II. HOLY SPIRIT

- Present your invitation for the Holy Spirit.
- Have everyone bow their heads and close their eyes.
- Ask how many children have received the Holy Spirit with the evidence of speaking with other tongues. Ask the children to raise their hands.
- Ask how many children do not have the evidence of speaking with other tongues and desire to have it.
- Ask those who raised their hand to stand by their chair.
- Ask the children who raised their hand to come down front.
- Build up the children who came forward.
- Take the children to another room.
- Take control when the children are in the counseling room.
- Build the children up.

- It is very important to screen the children by asking them the following questions:

- "Why did you come back here?" You are trying to locate if they know what they are doing. "Do you have Jesus into your heart, or are you born again?" It is very important the children are born again. If they are not Born again, but want to be filled with the Holy Spirit, have someone pray the Prayer of Salvation with them.

III. COUNSEL BEFORE PRAYER

- When you pray for the Holy Spirit, our Father will give to us **(Luke 11:11-14).**
- If you want to be filled with the Holy Spirit, you will be filled today!
- The Holy Spirit will come into our spirit. He gives us the words to speak. They are in our hearts; but WE need to speak them.
- We will not understand the words with our heads.

- We speak the words out of our mouth.

IV. PRAYING with CHILDREN for the HOLY SPIRIT

- Tell the children that you will pray for them.
- Start praying in tongues when finished.
- Lay hands on the children and encourage them.
- Thank God the Father for giving us Jesus.
- Ask the Father for the Holy Spirit to come to the children
- Thank the Holy Spirit for giving us the words to speak.
- Make sure each child pray in tongues out loud.
- Never allow a child to leave without the confidence and evidence of the infilling of the Holy Spirit. Listen to your heart for special counsel.

V. SCRIPTURES TO USE

- Mark 16:17
- Acts 1:4-5

How to Utilize Your Children's Ministry

- Acts 2:1-4
- 1Corinthians 14:2
- 1Corinthians 14:14
- Jude 20

LEADERSHIP GUIDELINES

1. A leader must set a quality example.
2. Communicate with your people. Let them know what is expected of them before they get involved.
3. Set attainable goals for your department.
4. Make sure everyone has something to do. (People become frustrated if they don't feel useful).
5. Be sensitive to individual needs. (Experienced people need to have more to do than inexperienced people).
6. Look for faithful workers.
7. Praise your people for doing a good job. (If all they hear

is correction, they won't feel they are doing anything right).
8. Delegate responsibility! A good leader doesn't do everything himself.
9. A good leader can always put himself in shoes of his subordinates.
10. A good leader never expects from his subordinates what he does not first expect from himself.
11. A good leader knows how to develop ability in others when there is nothing to be seen on the surface.
12. A good leader always has the interest of his people at heart.

How to Utilize Your Children's Ministry

Section Four

How to Utilize Your Children's Ministry

How to Utilize Your Children's Ministry

EVANGELISM MINISTRY

I believe with all my heart that God desires to use children to help reach the lost. In most of our churches however, kids are not really involved in any ministry at all. If we say that God can't use kids, we cut out one third to one-half of our work force. The time is too short to make such a mistake. God needs every available soldier in His army to bring in this last harvest.

The truth is that kids can open doors that adults can't. Some people would listen to a child share the gospel, while they would harden their hearts toward another adult.

TRAINING

A half hour to an hour is devoted to teaching and training before we go out. We go over the tract, practiced on each other and then we go on the streets and to parks. The kids go as observers the first three to four times, then are allowed to share. One adult is assigned two to three kids, never any more. It can seem like a crowd covering on the person if there is more than that.

Start the kids talking, present the Good News and then let them say the prayer with the one that has just been witnessed to. The results are amazing and the kids get so excited. One thing you must keep in mind with children is to be flexible, yet focused. They can flow with the Holy Ghost very easily, but children always need guidance and training.

REQUIREMENTS

These are the requirements set up for C.O.T.M. (Children on the Move). Adhere to these closely; but remember there's always room for exception when a child knows there's a call on his life.

1. Born again and Spirit filled, with the evidence of speaking in other tongues.
2. Nine (9) years or older.
3. A heart towards people and their eternal destiny.
4. A teachable spirit. Must be submitted to authority.
5. You must have a commitment to prayer.

The child has to be one who says they want to be in the C.O.T.M. – not the parents. The parents can tell you of the child's interest or how they have heard them pray for souls, but ultimately it has to be the child who wants to.

PRAY

Ask God to let you see the heart of children and the gifts within as you approach them. It will start out with a few and as the others hear of the experiences, they will get excited and want to join to. Have an orientation meeting to let the kids and parents know the requirements and commitment. Share the vision and what they will encounter on the streets. Be very honest about what's out there; but be sure to share what God's heart is for the lost. The parents should also be committed to prayer. They are putting their children on the front line and they must be alert to the enemy and keep their children under the blood.

HIT THE STREETS

Three hours on Saturday morning should be devoted to C.O.T.M. The adult leaders will meet from 9:30 a.m. to 10:30 a.m. to discuss upcoming events, problems, the Word God is giving for that day and to pray and intercede for the ministry. The kids will come at 10:30 a.m. There is a general discussion time in which the ministry should go over any upcoming events and what the leaders may have gotten in prayer. Team and location assignments are made. This is the time when the members of the ministry should get together and pray and go on the streets for a couple of hours.

Children's evangelism should be a fun time coupled with learning time. Remember, if the kids are not involved, they will usually lose interest.
When the wintertime arrives, it is strongly suggested that street ministry be limited to one or two days. This is not the time to stop ministering. One day should be for

teaching, and one day for fun activities such as roller-skating, bowling or movies. Make evangelism a lifestyle by witnessing at the same time while having fun.

EVANGELISM THROUGH PRACTICAL SERVICE

The kid's service should be oriented. If the church is having a cleanup day, the evangelism teams should participate. Take dinners to people around the holidays; let the children bring them to the door. Kids need to experience the blessing and warmth of God's love when they give of themselves to someone else. In this way, they will be planting seeds of love and doors will open up for them to share Jesus.

TEACHING TOOLS

Below are some practical suggestions, materials and scriptures to use for teaching your new evangelists:

1Timothy 4:11-16 – These things command and teach. [12]Let no man despise thy youth; but be thou an example of the believers, in word, in conversation,

in charity, in spirit, in faith, in purity. ¹³Till I come, give attendance to reading, to exhortation, to doctrine. ¹⁴Neglect not the gift that is in thee, which was given thee by prophecy, with the laying on of the hands of the presbytery. ¹⁵Meditate upon these things; give thyself wholly to them; that thy profiting may appear to all. ¹⁶Take heed unto thyself, and unto the doctrine; continue in them: for in doing this thou shalt both save thyself, and them that hear thee.

Matthew 5:13a	1Timothy 2:24-25
Matthew 28:19-20	1Timothy 3:14-15
Mark 16:15-20	1Timothy 4:5
John 13:35	Titus 2:1
Acts 1:8	Titus 2:15
1Corinthian 2:4-5	1Peter 3:15
1Corinthian 4:15	1John 4:15-17
1Corithian 5:9b; 11a	1Thessalonians 5:16-24
1Corithian 6:7	Colossians 2:6-7
1Corithian	Colossians

How to Utilize Your Children's Ministry

9:13	3:23
Philippians 2:13	Colossians 4;5-6

These scriptures are countless. Ask God to show you new ones all the time that pertain to children and witnessing. Use illustrations and involve the kids in teaching as much as possible. The following are some suggestions:

- **Get a silver bowl and silver cleaner.** Make sure the bowl is real tarnished. Put a label on the silver cleaner that says "the water of the Word." Teaching: We are tarnished and only the Blood of Jesus and His Word will make us clean. **(Philippians 1:9-10).** Proceed to clean the bowl with a cotton ball and silver cleaner. Watch out! It smells. So does our sin!

- *Gift Box:* Inside are the promises of God. Let the kids draw them out. You will need a white cloth colored with black magic marker. Dip it in bleach and watch the black color lift off. Let each child have a piece of cloth ad write down the one area where they want complete victory in their lives. Put the cloth in the bleach (which is also the water of the Word) and let them watch the Word dissolve that sin. The next week they will have to come to class with the promise from the Word of God they will claim and confess to build faith and have victory.

- **Take a needle, thread, and material.** A needle must always go straight. You can make it go up or down, left or right; but it still has to go straight. The needle is the Word of God. The thread is our walk with Jesus. The material is our life. Look up the Isaiah scripture where the writer talks about not going to the left or the right.

- Give a lesson on what kind of objections they could come up against on the streets. Ask the kids which scriptures would combat these objections.

- **Have them write out their own prayer that they would pray with someone.** Challenge everyone to share Jesus with one person in the next two weeks and share what their experience was.

- ***Do a teaching using lights*** to show that we are to shine everywhere for Jesus as we are His light to the world.

- ***Crepe paper and different treasures that represent spiritual truths.*** Make a crepe paper ball and wrap these things inside. Make several and let the kids unwrap them and tell what each treasure represents.

- ***Build a Lego model from an instruction book.*** Provide the identical pieces and have a couple of kids come forward and try to build that exact same model. Give them the book to work from after a few minutes. The model is us. The book is the Word of God. The pieces are scriptures to help us grow up in the faith.

- Do a skit that shows why people turn out the way they do by the confession of the mouth and agreement of two on the earth.

- ***Send out a monthly newsletter to the kids and their parents*** with the next month's schedule and prayer request and outings to take place.

- ***Keep your witnessing day regularly.*** Kids love to have a set time that they go out and witness. Always stress that this should be an everyday occurrence.

- ***Write down the names of everyone you pray with and put them in a fishbowl.*** Let the kids take a handful of names home with them to pray over within the next week. Learning comes from being with the Father and seeking His will for the children. He is our best and only source for plans to be carried out for his Kingdom and bringing in the harvest.

THREE BASIC PURPOSES

1. ***Ministry to the puppeteers.***
   The main reason for the puppets is to train kids for the ministry. Building character, commitment, and faithfulness into the children is a

whole lot more important than how good the puppet skits are.

2. ***Ministry to the Kidz for Jesus***
   We train the puppeteers that their number one reason for being on the puppet team is to minister to the kids in Children's Church.

3. ***Ministry to the community.***
   A puppet team is a great tool for outreach to schools, malls, nursing homes, and other churches.

How to Utilize Your Children's Ministry

How to Utilize Your Children's Ministry

Puppet

How to Utilize Your Children's Ministry

Ministry

BEGINNING YOUR PUPPET MINISTRY

1. There are many "nuts and bolts" steps in starting an effective puppet ministry. However, before you begin to take those steps in the natural, it is vitally important that you establish and maintain a spiritual foundation for success.
2. First, prayerfully consider and act on the four areas which follow; **"and you will cut through and make firm and plain and smooth, straight paths for your feet…" (Hebrews 12:13 Amplified)** as you step out and begin your puppet ministry.

3. What is your vision for the puppet ministry? Where there is no vision the people perish. **(Proverbs 29:18)**

4. Who will you minister to? What direction will you take? Pray and

earnestly seek God for His will to be done in your puppet ministry.

5. Share your vision. And the Lord answered me, and said write the vision, and make it plain upon tablets, that he may run that readeth it. **(Hebrews 2:2)**

6. Your pastor and staff members will be your best support system as long as you are open, up front and communicate with them from the beginning.

7. Bring in a high-quality performance puppet team to minister to the congregation. This is one of the best tools you can use in establishing a corporate understanding of the difference between entertainment and ministry.

8. Commitment. Yet the Lord is faithful, and He will strengthen (you) and set you on a firm foundation and guard you from the evil (one) **2Thessalonians 3:3 (Amplified).**

9. Set up goals and guidelines. Invite interested teens, children, parents

and adults to apply for joining the team. Those chosen should be motivated and encouraged by the corporate goals of the puppet tea. Make sure there is a commitment from each individual so that future misunderstandings will be avoided.

10. A six-week trial period, followed by a personal interview will help in establishing those who are truly interested in the ministry an allow a graceful out for those who are not ready or the commitment.

11. Ministry – not only to the multitudes; but to the puppeteers.

12. Jesus ministered to His twelve disciples in a different way than He did the multitudes. Train up puppeteers in the Word and in service.

AMBASSADORS FOR CHRIST

Puppet ministry is not just for entertainment. It is a minister with a purpose and a message presented in a special way. It communicates the gospel in a simple way, making it easy for people to understand and accept.

ALLOW GOD TO MINISTER TO YOU IN THE FOLLWING AREAS:

P ray individually and as a group. Share scriptures, hymns and psalms.
U nity and walking in love toward each other stops division.
P erformance materials. Research to fit your ministry needs.
P lan for excitement – outings, parties and get togethers.
E ncourage feedback and input from the puppeteers and sponsors.
T each other's by your example. Do not be just a hearer of the Word; be a doer.

T ry to keep everyone busy. Use your time wisely.
E arn the respect of those working with you and for each other.
A ttitude – Check it out!
M inister on all occasions with the love and understanding of Jesus.

M orals and appearance are important to you ad those you minister to.

I nsist o togetherness – avoid clichés at all costs – this is a group effort.
N egative comments cause hurt spirits; always use positive reinforcement.
I is not an important as we and you.
S tretch yourself by performing often enough; but avoid burn out.
T ake your team on the road. It will unify you.
R ecognition and reward = long-term commitment.
Y ou are serving God, who is a rewarder of faithfulness and diligence.

PRACTICAL PUPPET TEAM TIPS

1. Observe those children who are faithful and committed to your church. A good way is to observe how committed their parents are. If their parents don't understand commitment, the child won't either.
2. Get the parents to commit with the child by signing an application form.
3. Establish a weekly practice.
4. Begin each practice with a time of prayer ad ministry.
5. Schedule regular times of ministry outside your church.

6. Decide on a team name and logo. T-shirts or uniforms help to boost morale ad unify the team.
7. Do fun things with your kids. Reward them for their hard work. Remember your number one ministry s to them.
8. Plan an annual puppet tour. This should be the highlight of the year.
9. Communicate. Send monthly letters to the puppeteers and their parents. Tell them about upcoming events, activities and performances.

PUPPET TEAM RULES AND GUIDELINES

1. Puppet practice is on a set schedule, the same day and time each week. Puppeteers must be at every practice ad on time!

2. If a puppeteer has to miss a practice, he must call the puppet coordinator before practice.

3. Three acceptable reasons for missing puppet practice are:

   a) If you are sick;
   b) If you are out of town; and

c) If you have a planned family activity.

4. Puppeteers are expected to minister in Children's Church service every Sunday.

5. Those puppeteers who are in seventh grade or age must attend at least one youth group service per week or whenever they meet.

6. Puppeteers must abide by the dress code for all services in which they are ministering.

7. Puppeteers are expected to set an example for the rest of Children's Church by participating in worship.

8. Puppeteers are only to be behind the puppet stage right before or during a puppet skit. If they are not doing a puppet skit, they should be sitting in Children's Church.

9. Puppeteers are responsible for putting any puppets and props away after the service.

10. There is no dating allowed among the puppeteers.

11. Puppeteers scheduled to minister at the Sunday morning service need to attend the scheduled practice the preceding week.

12. Failure to abide by any of the guidelines could result in suspension from the puppet team.

How to Utilize Your Children's Ministry

MUSIC MINISTRY

STARTING and DEVELOPING a PRAISE TEAM

How to Start

Seek ye first the kingdom of God and His righteousness and all these things will be added unto you. (Matthew 6:33)

Priorities are Important
Set guidelines for your people so they have knowledge of the difference between ministry and performance and that their purpose is to put God out front, not themselves.
Everything is done to get people to the highest place with God and allow the Holy Spirit to manifest.

Teach the Word
Teach the children that the love of God is your priority so that the ministry will be pure.

SELECTING CHILDREN

How to Utilize Your Children's Ministry

Praise God for small beginnings! We started with a boom box, one singer and a drummer. Select children who are worshippers, an hold pitch and whose parents are faithful and committed to the church. Ask the parents first if they are able to get their children to the practices, etc. Make sure the children want to minister and that it's not just the desire of the parents for them to minister. Remember, you can start small and build a praise and worship team.

Section Five

How to Utilize Your Children's Ministry

FILES

A "traveling" file box works to organize your music, with files of:

- Praise and worship weekly lists
- Song lists and keys
- New songs
- Chord books and song books
- Equipment – warranties
- Paper
- Transparencies
- Words from the Lord
- CDs

PROMOTING UNITY

Plan some activities (ice cream or swimming parties, etc.) Bring your children little surprise gifts and have fun with them.

DON'T FORGET THE HOLY GHOST

Share the Word with your children and pray with them. Ask if they have needs or prayer requests. Let them pray! Explain some of the ways the Holy Ghost has ministered to you and let them tell of their experiences with God. Worship before or after the practice so they learn the difference between practice and worship. Pray for your children, pastor them and care.

Be open to the promptings of the Holy Ghost. He will give you great ideas because He is the Creator! He will also give you different ways to flow in the Spirit and things to say about the songs that will lift up Jesus.

Whatever you do let it be done to the Glory of God!

CHILDREN'S CHURCH SONG LEADER GUIDELINES

Your job is to lead the children into worship. God created us to worship Him and He is our first priority. Your job is extremely important because you are training these children in their first priority which is spending time with God.

Most people do not think children can really worship God; but the Bible states: **out of the mouth of babes and suckling's thou has perfected praise...** (Matthew 21:16).

How to Utilize Your Children's Ministry

Children will worship God if worship is presented at their level. Many children think that worship is something for mom and dad to do.

1. Always ask the minister if there are any special instructions she might want to give, how long praise service she wants, or if she may want singing while ministering to the sick, etc.

2. Always have the children stand for fast songs. Have the children sit for slow worship songs.

3. Be a bundle of joy. Your spirit will rub off on them.

4. Do everything you do with confidence and authority. Act like you know exactly what you are doing even if you don't feel like it.

5. Always sing songs in this order: fast songs, medium songs, slow songs.

6. If the children are not with you in singing or worship, stop and get

them with you. Don't just keep going.

7. Be sensitive to the children. They have a short attention span. This applies to worship as well as teaching.

8. Go from one song to the next without stopping. Keep the flow.

9. Keep your eyes open at all times.
    a. Yu need to see what's going on.
    b. Pastor can get your attention.

10. Do not talk. Your job is to leading SINGING! Exceptions are: "Would you please stand," or "Give the Lord a hand," or "I can't hear you," or "You may be seated."

11. Practice your song service at home to make sure it flows from fast to medium to slow songs.

12. After leading the children in worship, glance towards the

pastor for any further instructions. She may want to worship some more or she may want to get into the sermon.

13. We encourage you to keep to the guidelines; but you can feel free to be different.

How to Utilize Your Children's Ministry

Prayer Ministry

PRAYER MINISTRY

A big part of my vision as a pastor is to see children learn to pray and enter the deeper things of the Spirit. This is almost impossible in a large group setting. Some children will want to enter in; but there will always be those that are not interested. You cannot force the Holy Ghost on anyone.

Praise the Lord; He put the same vision in one of my assistant's heart. This particular assistant has attended the Prayer Intercessor School. She shared with me one day her desire to have the children pray more and lead prayer on Wednesday nights.

The following pages are filled with vital information in starting a children's prayer group.

Requirements for Children's Prayer Group

1. ***Commitment.*** Receive a signed commitment from parents and children to be there and be on time.

2. ***The Holy Ghost.*** Children need to be filled with the Holy Ghost with the evidence of speaking in other tongues.

3. ***Encouragement.*** Encourage the children to come "prayed up" (pray 5-10 minutes in tongues while they are coming to church).

4. ***Develop and Train.*** If you see some children that seem to be more mature, make a closed group. (Jesus chose 12 to specially train). It is wisdom not to inform parents your reasons for selecting out and closing a group. You can just inform them that the group is getting too large.

How to Utilize Your Children's Ministry

How to Utilize Your Children's Ministry

USHERS MINISTRY

Overview

The usher ministry involves the children in the ministry of helps. By involving them in a ministry which is relatively easy and with limited responsibility, it hopefully will instill in them the desire to be involved in children's Church and help prepare them for other ministries. This opportunity opens the door to nurture and train the children to serve the Lord.

Purpose

The usher's ministry has four-fold purpose:

1. To pastor the children in a smaller group setting; which may not be possible in the larger Children's Church environment.
2. To provide a ministry opportunity for the children, especially kids new to the idea of serving the Lord and ministering to others.

3. Develop leadership qualities in the children, especially with those children who hold the position of head usher or assistant head usher.
4. To provide the ministry of helps.

Parental Support

It is very important to have the parents understand what this ministry is all about. It is necessary to have their support to help the children learn to be responsible in fulfilling their role as an usher. This will be most evident in two areas: being on time on their scheduled days and making substitute arrangements if they cannot be there. If the parents display a lack of concern about schedules and responsibilities, the child will be hard to fulfill their duties.

Head Ushers and Assistant Head Ushers

To develop the ushering team, it is necessary to appoint a head usher and an assistant head usher for each service. These two positions have various responsibilities to perform for each service.

Below is a job description for the two positions.

These positions should be filled withholder children and preferably be those who you believe are more responsible and reliable. A child should "earn" these positions by serving faithfully in regular usher role. If possible, these positions should be set for each service; i.e., one individual should be serving each week with a break every 4-5 weeks. The assistant head usher should also serve weekly with an occasional break. Occasionally have an assistant head usher as head usher and have an usher serve as an assistant head usher. This will help to train them for advancement in the ministry. This regular scheduling should help the children to develop the feeling of responsibility toward their respective roles.

Scheduling
The number of ushers that you will need per service depends upon how many children are attending the services and how you handle the collection of the offering. The biggest single responsibility for the ushers is to take the offering.

The scheduling of your regular ushers is simply a matching of your available children in the ministry with the number of ushers required over the month for all the services. A monthly schedule should be made up and distributed to each usher. This schedule lays out each service for the month and the ushers who are on duty. Also, use a weekly schedule and update it each week. This schedule show is scheduled for the current week's services. This schedule makes it more convenient for the head usher to make "head checks" and notations of children who are absent or late.

Accountability
An accountability system should be established for making sure the children are participating when they are scheduled. Each usher is responsible to arrange for their own replacement in the event they cannot make a scheduled service. If a child is not able to accept this responsibility and does not fulfill the schedule dates consistently, the child should be given a warning. If it continues, you may need to dismiss them from the staff. Obviously, this situation is an ideal setting to pastor the child before dismissal.

Recognition
The ushers should be "set apart" from the other children an recognized as ushers. Using user pins or badges is a good way to do this. Reserved usher seats will help them in performing their duties. This helps reinforce the concept that they are part of the

service at the same time providing a ministry to the other kids.

New Recruits
Each child who has an interest in the usher ministry should fill out an usher application. This form briefly explains the usher ministry and the usher guidelines. Parents must sign this application, pledging their support to the ministry. Age minimum of 8 years old is suggested.

Once accepted, the new recruit should receive an usher packet. This should include:

    a. Welcome Letter
    b. Current Schedule
    c. Current List of Ushers
    d. Responsibility of the Usher's Guidelines Sheet

Ministry of Helps
The basic function of the ushering ministry is to provide the ministry of helps. This can be patterned after the usher's ministry within the adult church. The areas that can be considered should include:

    a. Take the offering during the church service.

b. Running errands for the pastor before the service begins.
c. Move equipment and ministry tools (whiteboards, overheads) as required during a service.
d. Monitoring children in their area and "modeling" proper behavior.
e. Ushering and greeting children as they come into service.

Meeting with the Ushers

If possible, the ministry head should meet with the ushers before each service. Praying as a group will help build the ministry awareness within the children. It will also build up the "ministry team" concept and draw the children into the ministry. Periodic usher meetings should be held. These meetings combine business and fun activities. Again, the idea is to make them feel a part of the ministry.

How to Utilize Your Children's Ministry

How to Utilize Your Children's Ministry

Audio Ministry

AUDIO VISUAL MINISTRY

The Audio Visual Ministry is responsible for setting up microphones and music for the Children's Church service. This ministry is an area of heavy responsibility because everything that is done during Children's church is dependent upon an effective sound system.

Anyone desiring to be involved in this ministry must first have permission from the children's pastor.

1. Must be able to work at least one service per week.
2. Must be at Children's Church one half hour before the service begins
3. The key to a good soundman is concentration. Always keep your eys o the pastor during the service. You never know when they might need extra microphones turned on or off.
4. Know what is coming up next. Anticipate.
5. No food or drink is allowed in the Audio Visual area.
6. After using CDs be sure to place them back in the exact same place where they belong.

How to Utilize Your Children's Ministry

7. Never play with the microphones during service. The equipment is very expensive.
8. CDs and DVDs are not to be removed from the AV department without pastor's permission.
9. You are responsible for the appearance of the AV area. Keep it clean and organized

Preparing for a Service

1. Set up two microphones.
2. Place wireless microphone with working battery installed on the pulpit.
3. Turn on amplifier and all sound equipment.
4. Check microphone levels.
5. Ask children's pastor for any puppet skit tapes that will be used during service.
6. Be sure to get a service schedule from children's pastor.
7. Select music for entry and offering.
8. After service put all microphones and stands away.
9. Be sure to turn all sound equipment off.

RESPONSE TO WORKERS APPLICATION

Thank you for your support of the Children's Ministry. You have a very pleasant surprise waiting for you. The children are very precious and loving and are growing each in the power of God and the knowledge of our Lord Jesus Christ.

Without the help of people like you, it is difficult for one or two people to minister to 50-100 children. These children are very fashionable and will believe and trust what you tell them. You will be helping us shape, mold, them more like Jesus each time you are in Children's Church.

Each department is different because the children are at different growth stages physically and spiritually. The Children's Ministry is designed to minister to each child on their level.

Children's Church gives the children a chance to do what they have been taught. They have an opportunity to be used by God in the ministry of helps in various areas. We believe in building upon a strong foundation built upon "The Rock," Jesus Christ.

We believe you will find your place in the Body of Christ. We appreciate your interest in this area of Children's Ministry. If you have any questions, pleae feel free to contact the Ministry Assistant Department Head or myself. We would like to help you in any way we can.

With sincere appreciation,

Elder Elizabeth Paddy
Children's Pastor
Victory Christian Center

How to Utilize Your Children's Ministry

Section Six

How to Utilize Your Children's Ministry

How to Utilize Your Children's Ministry

How to Utilize Your Children's Ministry

The purpose of this section is simply this: to have *fun*. Kids (and adults) need to laugh and play! Let these games be a part of your weekly children's ministry. Kids of all ages will enjoy these high-energy games. So...start the timer, play the music and let the fun begin!

GAME NO. 1
THE BALLOON STOMP

Object of the game: to see who can put the memory verse in the correct order.
It is an excellent way for the children to learn the memory verse.

Materials: Balloons; Paper; Pens

How to play: Select players. The amount depends on how long the scripture is. Write the memory verse on a piece of paper and cut it into pieces. Put the pieces into the balloon. The children will stomp the balloon to get the piece of paper.

GAME NO. 2
DUCT HEAD

Object of the game: to see which player gets the most objects stuck on his head.

Materials: Duct tape and various objects such as candy, etc.

How to play: Select several players. Wrap the duct tape around their head with sticky side out. Put various objects on the floor. Players get on their knees with their hands behind their backs and try to pick up the objects with their heads. The player with the most objects stuck to his head wins.

GAME NO. 3
HANGIN DONUTS

Object of the game: to eat the donut off the string without it falling to the ground.

Materials: Donuts; String; Clothes racks

How to Play: Select two players. Use the string to hang two donuts from the clothes rack. Without using their hands, players begin to eat the suspended donut as fast as they can without if falling off the string. When the time is up, the player who has eaten the most or all of the donut wins.

GAME NO. 4
HULA RELAY

Object of the game: to see who's balloon will pop first.

Materials: 2 large hula hoops; balloons; and 2 jump ropes

How to Play: Select 2 players and position them in front of a jump rope, hula hoop and balloon.
On go, the players will jump rope around the room one time. They will hula hoop 8 times and then blow up the balloon. The first balloon to pop wins.

How to Utilize Your Children's Ministry

Section Seven

ACKNOWLEDGEMENTS

No achievement in life is without the help of many known and unknown individuals who have impacted our lives. We owe every measure of our success to the array of input from so many. Here are just a few who made this work possible:

- To my Bishop, my Spiritual Dad, and my mentor Jimmie A. Ellis III, who allowed me to flow freely in Children's Ministry. Thank you for your unwavering support.

- To my son, Ryan Gore, for allowing your mom to pursue her passion and purpose.

- Rhonda Taggart, Monica Harmon, Josey Williams Mary Ellen Lavender, Betty Bellamy and D'Adrian Leach.

How to Utilize Your Children's Ministry

- To the Kidz for Jesus Ministry at Victory Christian Center who allowed me the privileged to develop, share, and test the ideas and principles in this book.

- Finally, I acknowledge and thank the Ultimate Children's Pastor of all Pastors, my Lord and Savior Jesus Christ, who himself established the standard for all Children's Pastors to measure up to. I am forever indebted and grateful to you for your eternal gift of life and for igniting within me the passion for children's ministry.

ABOUT THE AUTHOR

Elizabeth Paddy is an author, teacher, and founder of I Have Nothing But Kids Ministry and Save the Children Outreach. She is a native of Washington, DC. She graduated from Benedict College with a Bachelor of Art Degree in Elementary Education. She is a seasoned professional with 25 years of teaching experience to her credit in the Trenton, New Jersey Public School District. She Pastors the Children's Ministry at Victory Christian Center (VCC) in Philadelphia Pennsylvania. She is the CEO and founder of C.O.N.F.I.D.E.N.T., which stands for "Children of New Found Faith and Individuality Delivering Extraordinary Next Level Triumph". Confident is an inspired animated character from her newly released book, entitled Say what God Says, Kids Faith Confessions. She serves as an Elder under the leadership of Bishop Jimmie A. Ellis III, at Victory Christian Center.

In 2003 she received the Light Award from Victory Christian Center. She was elected New Jersey Governor's Teacher of the Year in 1999 and again in 2008 for Excellence in Teaching. She received the Staff Administration Faithfulness Award (SAFA). In 2009 she received VCC Creativity Award. In December, 2009 she received the Best Department Head Award for outstanding leadership and service to Victory Christian Center. She received in June, 2009 the Outstanding Service Award.

Elizabeth Paddy has published several nationally published books including *Say What God Says, Kids Faith Confessions and Affirmations for the Confident Kid.* She is also a profound speaker divinely led by God and have recorded CDs on various topics including *How to Keep Kids on the Edge of Their Seat; Making a Difference in Children's Ministry; Giants in the Life of Kids; I Have Nothing but Kids; Utilizing*

How to Utilize Your Children's Ministry

Your Children's Ministry and *What About the Children.*

Often referred to as Liz, she takes great pride in making children laugh. She is a passionate teacher and enjoys making children enthusiastic about learning. Whether her teaching tool is through, playing high-energy games or simply the direct one-to-one attention of a compassionate teacher to her students. She has achieved immeasurable accomplishments with students and parents alike.

Her mission is to let every child know that they are a winner and not a loser. She is the mother of one son who's destined for greatness; and a grandmother of three wonderful grandchildren.

To contact **Elizabeth Paddy** *or for more information please email:*

elizabethpaddy@yahoo.com

Or call

How to Utilize Your Children's Ministry

(215) 421-5902

You are invited to send your prayer requests.

How to Utilize Your Children's Ministry

www.ingramcontent.com/pod-product-compliance
Lightning Source LLC
Chambersburg PA
CBHW071123090426
42736CB00012B/1994